CHART HITS OF 2010-2011

ISBN 978-1-61780-770-1

HAL•LEONARD® CORPORATION
7777 W. BLUEMOUND RD. P.O. BOX 13819 MILWAUKEE, WI 53213

Visit Hal Leonard Online at
www.halleonard.com

BACK TO DECEMBER

Words and Music by
TAYLOR SWIFT

Moderately

I'm so glad you made time to see me.

How's life? Tell me, how's your fam - 'ly? I have - n't seen _

them in ___ a while. ___

You've been ___ good, bus-i-er than ev - er. Small talk,

work and the weath - er. Your guard ___ is up ___ and I ___ know why. ___

___ Be - cause the last time

I _____ go back to De - cem - ber all _____ the time. ___

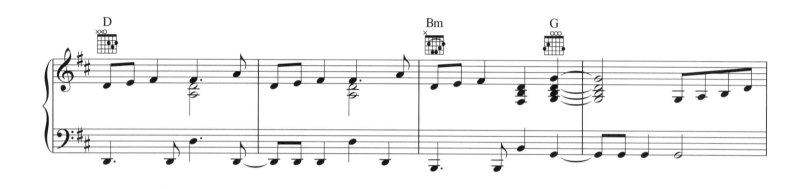

These days I have - n't been sleep - in'; stay - in' up, play - in' back

BEG STEAL OR BORROW

Words and Music by
RAY LaMONTAGNE

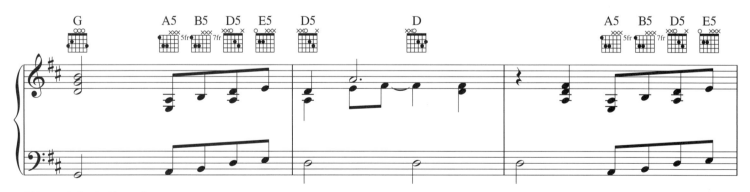

* Recorded a half step lower.

gon - na make a stand. _ You beg, steal, _ you bor - row. _

You beg, you steal, _____ you bor - row. _

Well,

D.S. al Coda

So the

CODA

Young ___ man, full of big plans __ and think-in' a-bout __ to-mor-

row; young ___ man, gon-na make a stand. __ You

EMPIRE STATE OF MIND

Words and Music by ALICIA KEYS, SHAWN CARTER,
JANE'T SEWELL, ANGELA HUNTE, AL SHUCKBURGH,
BERT KEYES and SYLVIA ROBINSON

Moderate Hip-Hop

* Recorded a half step higher.

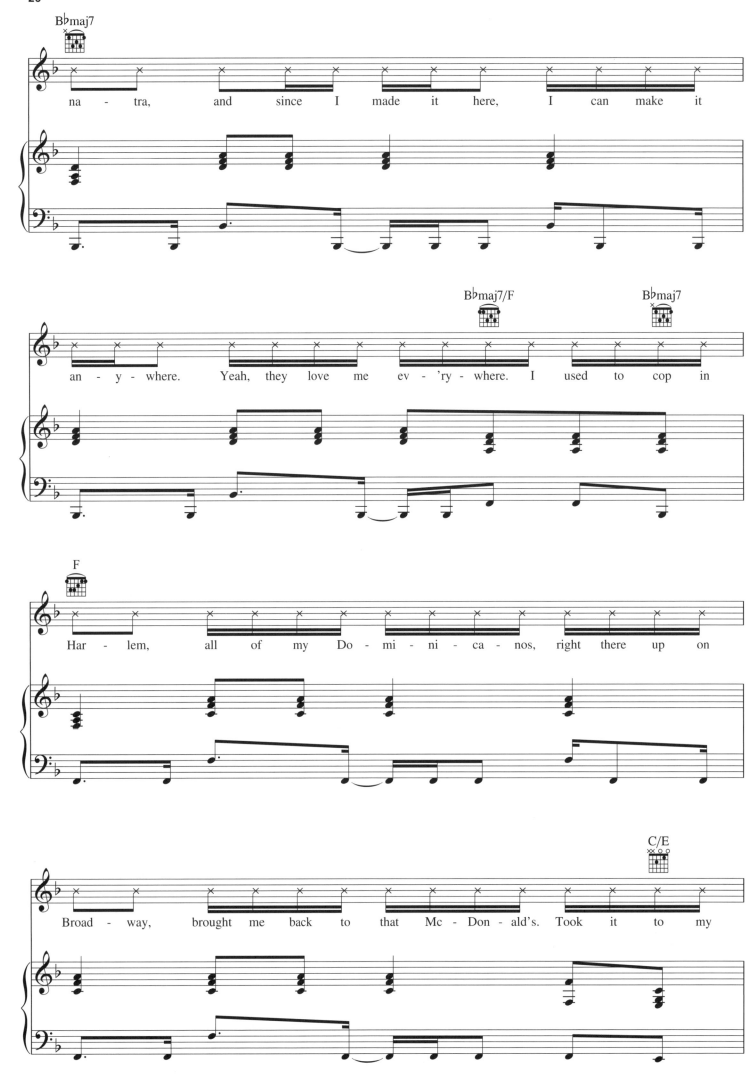

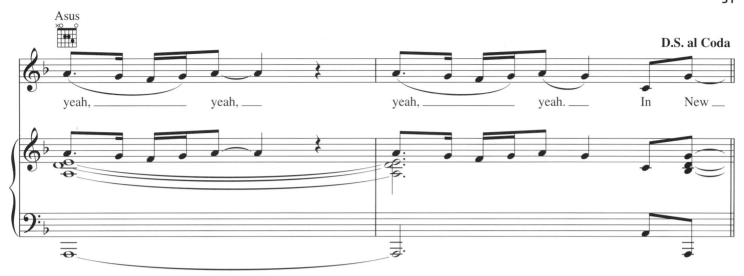

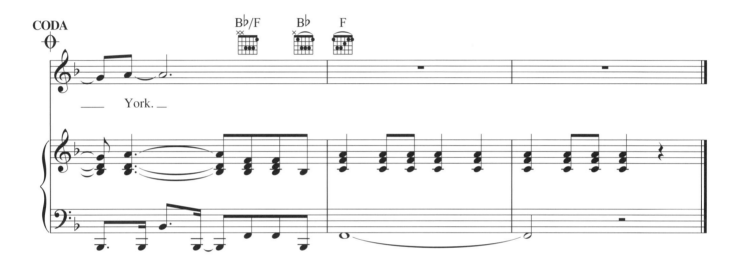

Rap Lyrics

2. Catch me at the X with OG at a Yankee game.
   Dude, I made the Yankee hat more famous than a Yankee can.
   You should know I bleed blue, but I ain't a crip though,
   But I got a gang of brothas walking with my clique though.

   Welcome to the melting pot, corners where we selling rocks,
   Afrika bambaataa, home of the hip-hop,
   Yellow cab, gypsy cab, dollar cab, holla back,
   For foreigners it ain't for they act like they forgot how to act.

   Eight million stories out there and they're naked.
   City, it's a pity half of y'all won't make it.
   Me, I gotta plug Special Ed, I got it made,
   If Jeezy's paying LeBron, I'm paying Dwyane Wade.

   3 dice, Cee Lo, 3-Card Monte,
   Labor Day parade, rest in peace Bob Marley.
   Statue of Liberty, long live the World Trade,
   Long live the King, yo, I'm from the Empire State that's...

3. Lights is blinding, girls need blinders
   So they can step out of bounds quick.
   The sidelines is blind with casualties, who sip your life casually,
   Then gradually become worse. Don't bite the apple, Eve.

   Caught up in the in-crowd, now you're in style,
   And in the winter gets cold, en vogue with your skin out.
   The city of sin is a pity on a whim,
   Good girls gone bad, the city's filled with them.

   Mami took a bus trip, now she got her bust out,
   Everybody ride her, just like a bus route.
   Hail Mary to the city, you're a virgin,
   And Jesus can't save you, life starts when the church in.

   Came here for school, graduated to the high life.
   Ball players, rap stars, addicted to the limelight.
   MD, MA got you feeling like a champion,
   The city never sleeps, better slip you a Ambien.

FIREWORK

Words and Music by MIKKEL ERIKSEN,
TOR ERIK HERMANSEN, ESTHER DEAN,
KATY PERRY and SANDY WILHELM

FORGET YOU

Words and Music by BRUNO MARS,
ARI LEVINE, PHILIP LAWRENCE,
THOMAS CALLAWAY and BRODY BROWN

GIVE A LITTLE MORE

Words by ADAM LEVINE
Music by ADAM LEVINE,
JESSE CARMICHAEL and JAMES VALENTINE

With a groove

Now you've been _ bad _ and it goes _ on _

_ and on _ and on _ 'til you come home, _ babe, _

ing, feel - ing noth - ing, won - der - ing if it will ev - er change.

Gm7

And then I give a lit - tle more, ooh, ____ ba -

Am7

- by, oh, ____ ____ give a lit - tle more, ooh ____ ba -

A7

- by, oh. ____ I'm not fall - ing in love ____ with you, I'm ____

Dm

THE HOUSE THAT BUILT ME

Words and Music by TOM DOUGLAS
and ALLEN SHAMBLIN

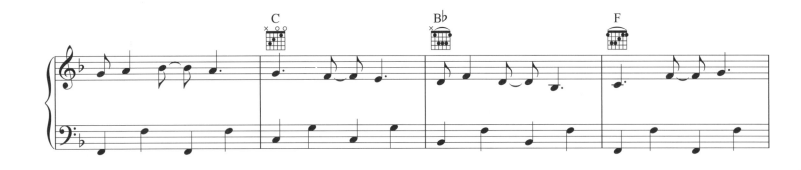

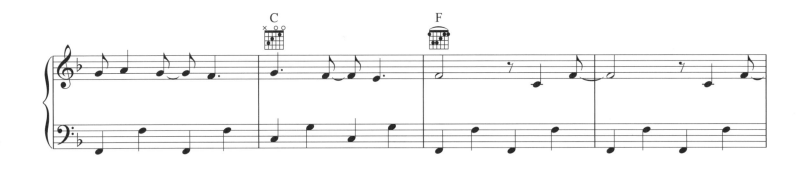

I know they say _____ you

JUST THE WAY YOU ARE

Words and Music by BRUNO MARS,
ARI LEVINE, PHILIP LAWRENCE,
KHARI CAIN and KHALIL WALTON

Moderate Hip-Hop groove

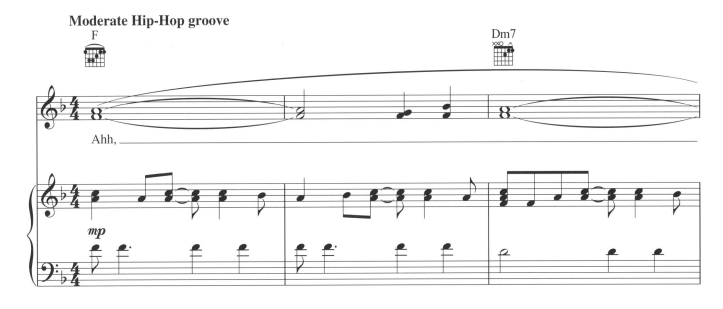

Ahh,

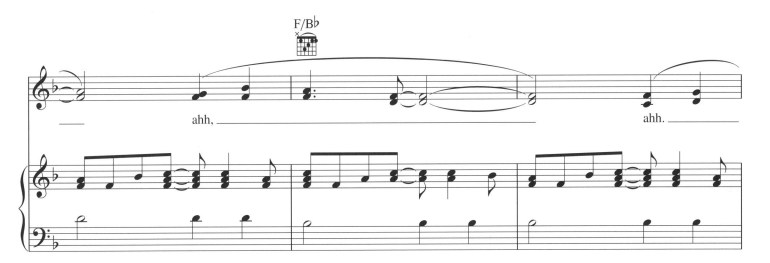

ahh, ahh.

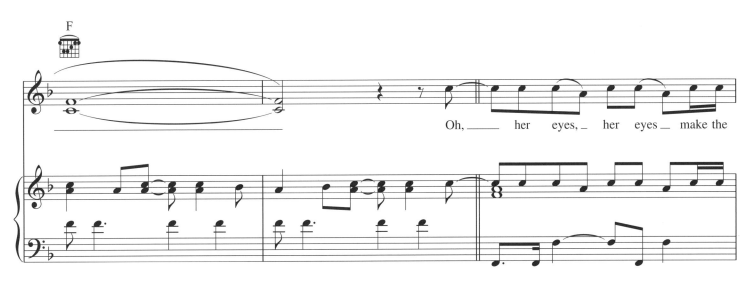

Oh, her eyes, her eyes make the

KING OF ANYTHING

Words and Music by
SARA BAREILLES

LITTLE LION MAN

Words and Music by
MARCUS MUMFORD

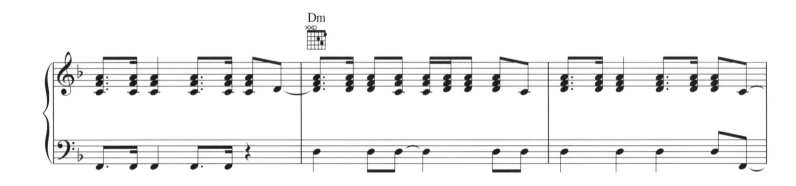

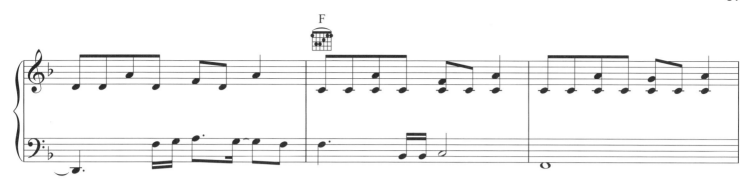

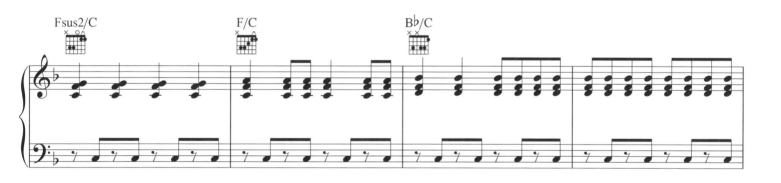

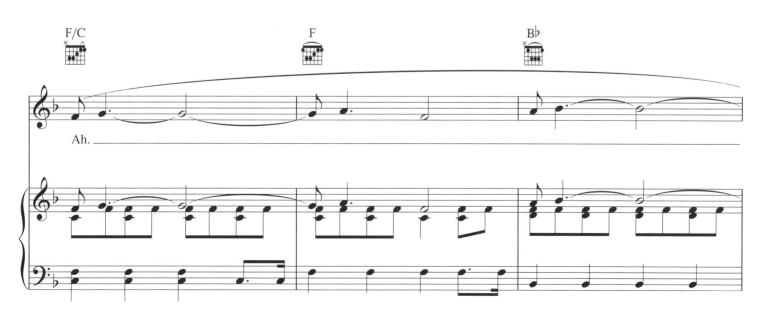

Ah.

MARRY ME

Words and Music by
PAT MONAHAN

MINE

Words and Music by
TAYLOR SWIFT

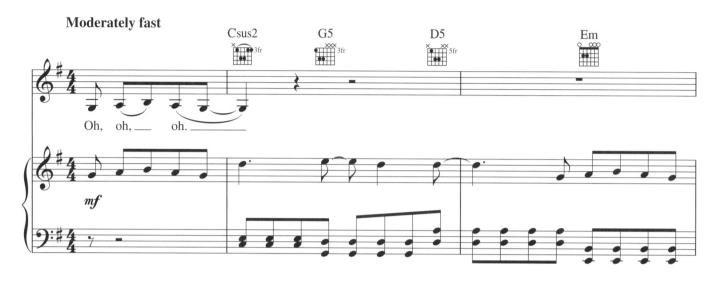

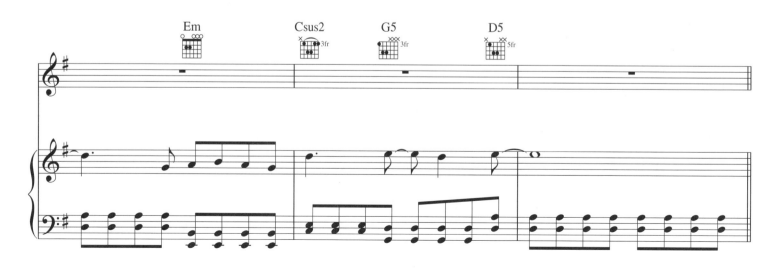

NOTHIN' ON YOU

Words and Music by BOBBY SIMMONS,
BRUNO MARS, ARI LEVINE
and PHILIP LAWRENCE

Raise Your Glass

Words and Music by ALECIA MOORE,
MAX MARTIN and JOHAN SCHUSTER

SECRETS

Words and Music by
RYAN TEDDER

This time — don't need an-oth-er per-fect line; — don't care if crit-ics ev-er jump in line. — I'm gon-na give all my se-crets a-way. —

My God, a-maz-ing how we got this far. It's like we're chas-in' all those stars who's driv-in' shin-y big black cars. And ev-'ry

SEPTEMBER

Words and Music by CHRIS DAUGHTRY
and JOSH STEELY

Moderate Country Rock

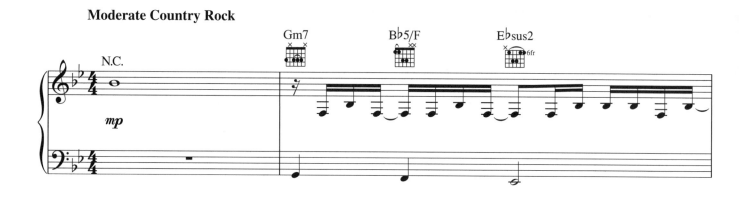

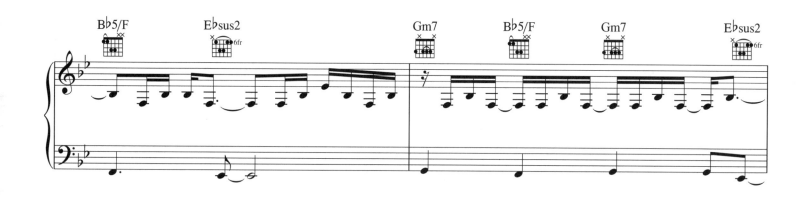

How the time passed _ a - way, _ all the
all seems _ so clear. _ There is

trou - ble that __ we gave __ and all those days __ we spent __ out by __ the lake. __
noth - ing left __ to fear. __ So we made our way __ by find - ing what __ was real. __

Has it all gone __ to waste, __ all the
Now the days are __ so long __ that __

prom - is - es __ we made? __ One by one __ they van - ish just __ the same. __
sum - mer's mov - in' on. __ Reach for some - thin' that's __ al - read - y gone. __

TEENAGE DREAM

Words and Music by LUKASZ GOTTWALD,
MAX MARTIN, BENJAMIN LEVIN,
BONNIE McKEE and KATY PERRY

Moderate Dance beat

You think I'm pret-ty with-out an-y make-up on, you think I'm fun-ny when I tell the punch-line wrong. I know you get me, so I let my walls come down, down.

WE R WHO WE R

Words and Music by KESHA SEBERT,
JOSHUA COLEMAN, BENJAMIN LEVIN,
LUKASZ GOTTWALD and JACOB KASHER HINDLIN

Moderate Dance groove

Additional Lyrics

Rap 1: Hot and dangerous, if you're one of us then roll with us.
'Cause we make the hipsters fall in love when we've got our hot pants on enough.
And, yes, of course, we does. We runnin' this town just like a club.
And, no, you don't wanna mess with us. Got Jesus on my necklace, uss, uss.

Rap 2: Turn it up. It's about damn time to live it up.
I'm so sick of bein' so serious. It's makin' my brain delirious.
I'm just talkin' truth. I'm tellin' you 'bout the shit we do.
We're sellin' our clothes, sleepin' in cars, dressin' it down, hittin' on dudes, hard.

WHAT'S MY NAME?

Words and Music by MIKKEL ERIKSEN,
TOR ERIK HERMANSEN, AUBREY GRAHAM,
ESTHER DEAN and TRACY HALE

Rap: *(See additional lyrics)*

Oh,